A Seniors' Guide to Making Money Online

Boost Your Monthly Income By Selling Digital and Tangible Products

RON KNESS

No part of this book may be reproduced, stored in a retrieval system, or transmitted in any form or by any means, electronic, mechanical, photocopying, recording, scanning, or otherwise, without the prior written permission of the publisher, except for the inclusion of brief quotations in a review.

This book is for **personal use only**.

Copyright © 2016 Ron Kness

All rights reserved.

ISBN-13: 978-1537625362

ISBN-10: 1537625365

Contents

Disclaimer 4

Introduction 5

Second Career for Senior Citizens 6

Picking a Niche That's Right for You 16

Getting Your Website Up and Running 24

Building a List of Loyal Subscribers 31

Blogging to Bring Visitors to Your Site 36

Reviewing Products as an Affiliate 41

Developing an Info Product to Sell 46

Recruiting Affiliates and Joint Venture Partners 53

Coaching Others in Exchange for Pay 58

Supplementing Senior Income as a Service Provide 62

Ways to Increase Traffic and Sales 67

Final Thoughts 73

About the Author 74

Disclaimer

This publication is for informational purposes only and is not intended as business advice. Business advice should always be obtained from a qualified business professional experienced in the type of business you are considering starting.

Every possible effort has been made in preparing and researching this material. We make no warranties with respect to the accuracy, applicability of its contents or any omissions.

Introduction

As a senior citizen, you have many experiences and interests that can serve you well in the world of Internet Marketing. Even without being a so-called "expert", your years and insights make you knowledgeable in many things and far surpass the younger generation's ability to lead an audience, because they do not yet have the life and work experiences that you do.

From life experiences, to how to solve a problem, to just about any topic you can think of, you have an audience just waiting to soak in the knowledge you have to offer. You might as well make some income off of it!

In this book, I show you how to get into the world of Internet marketing by buying a domain name, signing up for hosting, getting traffic either paid or free, so that your offer gets seen and of course make sales.

If you are new to this type of marketing, then start small at first. Just start out getting one website up and running. From there you may decide to stay with just one site and not create others. Some people are happy with the income one site can bring in. Or if you want, you can purchase more domain names, get a larger hosting package if necessary and create many websites. The choice is yours. So why not get started!

Second Career for Senior Citizens

Seniors today are coming out of retirement with energy and excitement for the next stage and possible second career of their lives. For many, it's an exciting time knowing they have the skills and the methods for developing their own businesses that will help them supplement the gross inadequacy of retirement savings or pensions.

But for many seniors, retirement is a time of disappointment and regret. They're disappointed because they didn't plan better for their retirement years and regret that they have to get at least a part time job to make ends meet.

Embarking on a second career for seniors isn't as daunting as it may seem. Now, with the powers of the Internet at their backs, seniors can learn new skills and build an Internet business they can use to supplement incomes and keep their minds sharp.

Benefits of Coming Out of Retirement as an Entrepreneur

Many seniors are realizing that what they've saved for retirement years isn't going to be enough to support them and even provide them with necessities – much less the luxuries they'd like to enjoy.

That's why so many seniors are building online businesses well before the retirement party. One of the benefits of building a part-time business in your spare time before you retire is that you'll already have an income and it can increase as your business grows.

Plus – having a second career to pursue after retirement keeps your mind sharp and you won't ever get bored if you're committed to your business pursuits. But this time you can set your own hours and only answer to yourself as the boss.

Starting an online business long before the retirement day comes is the best way to begin enjoying your business and reaping the benefits before you actually need them to kick in.

You'll get to know how far the skills (or hobbies) you already have will take you in your business endeavors and just what will be required to grow the business when you finally have more hours in the day to devote to it.

Beginning a new business on the "net" may not be for all seniors. It may take developing a completely different mindset and lots of patience to succeed than what you are used to. A realistic way to look at beginning any new business is that it will take six months to a year to know if you're going to succeed fully at it.

Most seniors think the idea of creating an online business plan is highly preferable to searching for a new job after retirement. Your hours and your life enjoy a flexibility that just can't be found in any other part-time or full-time job.

When you consider that most in the baby boomer generation will not have a pension they can rely upon or have enough money saved for a long retirement, the outlook can be bleak, except for the possibilities of making money and beginning a new career after retirement age.

The Internet has made it possible to redefine the retirement years for seniors. No matter how old you are, you can learn what it takes to become an online entrepreneur and use it to build a business even before retirement.

Rethink the concept of retirement and learn how you can benefit from starting an online business – even before you retire.

Why More Seniors Are Launching an Online Business

Supplementing a totally inadequate retirement income is a major concern for those who are retired or about to enter their retirement years. Another concern is keeping themselves mentally and physically active during years when some are willing to just relax and do nothing – causing both mental and physical atrophy.

Also, launching an online business has become very appealing to those who lack money for startup costs of a brick and mortar business and who want to avoid headaches and time involved in an offline business.

The cost of starting an online business after the computer and Internet connection costs are minimal. Plus, seniors can turn a passion, such as golfing or fishing into money-making blogs, websites and businesses offering products either digital, tangible or both.

There's no overhead such as advertising unless you want to invest in paid methods. When you know how to use the Internet for profit, you can advertise for free on social media and other sites.

Those who have developed useful skills are way ahead of the retirement game. For example, if you've been a counselor, you can begin a self-help site, teach an online course or write a book for Kindle or for Amazon's print-on-demand site CreateSpace.

There are many ways for seniors to begin new and exciting careers on the Internet and make a supplemental income to help pay for necessities or luxuries that the retirement income won't cover.

Many seniors are ready to kick back and enjoy some leisure activities they've been unable to do during their job years. An Internet business allows you to set your own hours and devote as much - or as little - time as needed or wanted to build your business to the level you desire.

Online businesses are also great for meeting new friends and socializing. Studies show that seniors who retire often miss the opportunity to interact with coworkers each day.

An online business opens the door to global networks, letting you get to know people from all walks of life and around the world.

And an online business is low stress. Compare the thought of running a business from the comfort of your home to beginning your new career by purchasing and running a restaurant, for example.

When you're entering your retirement years, the last thing you want to do is immerse yourself in a high-stress, high-investment type of business. With an online business, you can begin slowly, with very little overhead needed.

Thanks to the power of the Internet, seniors can now supplement their retirement incomes by starting an online business that they can be proud of and one which will provide satisfaction for many years to come.

What's the Learning Curve for Senior Online Entrepreneurs?

Some seniors are lucky enough to have learned basic computer and Internet skills at previous jobs, while others are clueless about how to maneuver in this highly technical world.

Many seniors shun computers and the Internet because they think it's too difficult and they're too old to learn and others think it's exciting and are eager to join the trend.

Learning to use a computer can be fun and even profitable for seniors if they have the right attitude.

The learning curve for seniors getting to know computers and use the Internet varies according to the knowledge they already have. Luckily, there are classes available, both on and offline to help anyone at any level learn from exactly the place they're at.

Online, step-by-step videos and written tutorials are available so that seniors can learn and progress at their own pace. When seniors are relatively comfortable with maneuvering around the "net", they may decide to start their own business to supplement retirement income or simply provide them with luxuries they can no longer afford.

Running an online business may seem like a formidable task if you're not familiar with many technical aspects of the Internet. The good news is that many tasks can be outsourced if you're not ready to tackle them.

Computers and the Internet can provide seniors with many hours of fun and socializing. It's a way to bring the world into the living room and keep them active, both mentally and socially without ever having to leave their homes.

Unlimited support is also available for those seniors who want to learn more about computers and the Internet. Once seniors learn that they can easily stay in touch with friends and family through emails, Skype, Facebook and chatting, they usually warm up to the idea of spending some time learning this incredible and fun opportunity.

Many seniors may lack confidence in themselves to learn such an intimidating new skill, but with the proper support, they usually begin to enjoy the process and want to learn more.

Some seniors have trouble learning the language of computers and the "net". There are so many technical terms which may be totally unfamiliar to them, but are part of most people's everyday language.

Learning the definition of terms such as URL address or web browsing may seem like learning a new language, but begin slowly and progress to the next level as you feel more comfortable.

Starting a Business for Under $12 a Month

Amazingly, that's typically all you're going to pay to start your new online business. A domain name is about $10 per year and hiring a hosting service is under $10 per month – but you usually have to pay for a year of hosting in advance, so the initial outlay is more. The remainder of tasks for your new business can be done by you – unless you choose to outsource some of the work (such as writing content).

More retirees are choosing to supplement their retirement incomes with an online business rather than enduring the astronomical costs of an offline business. The cost is low and they can set their own hours and be their own boss.

All you need are a computer and an Internet connection and some knowledge of both and you're ready to go. There are so many types of online business which utilize the skills and experiences that seniors likely have that it can be fairly easy to find a niche that will be profitable and even fun and rewarding.

Most of the technical knowledge that seniors may not be familiar with can be outsourced for very little money – or enlist the help of children and grandchildren to help you out. Unlike a traditional offline business, the requirements of an online business are as simple as having an idea and developing a blog and website.

More than anything else, starting an online business requires discipline. If you're used to working for a boss, you may find it difficult to set your own hours and work at your own pace – but with patience and fortitude, you can make it work.

You also have to remember that there is a lot of competition in online businesses. Your consumers will be looking for quality and value and your job is to convince them that your product is what they need.

That can be accomplished with researching of your niche and offering the highest quality product you can possible provide. Never cut corners when it comes to quality and always take the high road when it comes to your customers.

Keep upgrading and updating your website and blog as you can afford it. Spending a bit more money to polish your website and create interesting content will drive traffic to your site and the result will be more sales and profit.

Types of Businesses You Can Launch Online

No matter what your skills or preference, there is likely an online business model that will appeal to you. If you're a senior just out of retirement, it's especially enticing to start another career or build your own business with very little startup costs and the pleasure of being your own boss.

Even if you don't know a great deal about computers or the Internet, you can catch up with one or more of the many courses – both online and offline – that will get you moving in the right direction.

The types of businesses from which you can choose are many and varied. Consider your skills and experience, and check out such business models as affiliate marketing, writing or recording info products, coaching or selling content (PLR) or even selling tangible items that get delivered directly to your customers door (called drop shipping, thus having to avoid stocking an inventory).

There are also ways to become a virtual assistant to a company or person or you could begin creating graphics for eBooks and other specialties.

If you have a knack for writing, you may want to consider ghostwriting or freelance writing where you write reports for businesses or blog posts for online business owners.

Free online tools are available and easy to implement and can be very powerful as a way to get you started. One of the top online demands for services on the Internet in 2016 include freelance writing.

As a freelance writer, you would write articles, content and possibly propose creative ideas for future work. Most large businesses and websites prefer to outsource their writing tasks on an as-needed basis, so there are enough freelance writing jobs for most everyone.

You may want to consider becoming a virtual assistant if you have experience in managing an office or projects. As a virtual assistant, you would help businesses and people stay organized and help them complete administrative tasks. Keep in mind that your list of tasks may vary according to your client's needs.

The growth of the Internet has made it possible for people to have a home-based business. This is the perfect scenario for retired seniors, those with disabilities that make it difficult to commute to a job or to those who desire to create their own businesses and leave a legacy they can be proud of.

Picking a Niche That's Right for You

When it comes to launching a career online, there are many reasons for pursing this line of work. You might just want a purpose in life – a reason to get up in the morning, the ability to start over fresh and do something you love in retirement.

But for many seniors, additional income is a heavy factor in their decision to get into online marketing, so you'll want to focus on a niche that combines personal satisfaction with income potential.

When you're looking at a niche based on profits, first consider whether there's a large enough audience for it or not. If you go too narrow, it might be harder to make money. Make sure it's a niche or demographic area that pays for information or tangible items, too.

Some niches lean heavily toward tire kickers (or bottom feeders as they are known in the business) – people unwilling to pay any money for advice or tips. They will gladly accept your freebie offer, but never buy anything from you.

Look on sites like Amazon or Barnes and Noble at the ratings of different books in your niche to see if people are buying books that explain the niche topic you are considering. The lower the placement, the better the book is selling. For example a good rating on Amazon would be placing #121 out of 2,163,459 books on that topic. The rating is usually found after the description of the book.

It's even more profitable if you can find a niche that combines tangible and digital products. A digital product might be a book on "losing weight with smoothies" while a tangible product might be the blenders that make the smoothies. In this example you could write a book on smoothies, and either add a chapter on blenders or write a small report that you could give away with your Amazon links to select blenders. When someone buys a blender through your link, you get a commission from it. Or you could include your Amazon links right in your eBook (called anchor links).

Anti-aging is a great niche that's profitable and perfect for seniors to get into. People want to know all sorts of information – such as protecting their memory, getting fit, how to keep wrinkles at bay, managing weight and more.

Of course, think of the tangibles that go along with a topic like that – there are thousands of products for anti-aging in the beauty, health and fitness categories alone. All you have to do is lead the way and guide them to the right products and pick up your commission along the way!

Picking a Niche That Makes You Happy

As a senior just getting into online marketing, keep in mind that you don't have to sacrifice enjoyment for a paycheck. You can merge your interests with profitability.

So let's say you're finally retired and can't wait to spend every day playing golf, by-the-way it sounds good now but the excitement will soon wear off.

You could start a niche golf site where you're giving tips and recommending certain courses or reviewing products on a regular basis. Amazon sells all sorts of golf equipment, clothing and trainers to learn how to play better that could earn you commissions.

Topics like fishing, knitting, cooking, and even saving your marriage are all hot sellers that might be interesting and profitable for you to tap into. There are hundreds of lucrative niches that would make you smile – so keep the things you enjoy in mind as you begin hunting a niche of your own that will bring happiness to your life. And you'll do a better job of writing, and have to do less research, if you write on topics you are experienced in and passionate about.

Picking a Niche Based on Your Knowledge

Some of you may have lifelong careers that you can now put into action online as an entrepreneur. Whether you were a mechanic, a plumber, a lawyer, or a teacher – there are people willing to pay for the information you share. The DIY or Do-It-Yourself is another hot niche. If you are good at writing step-by-step instructions, this could be a niche to get into.

You can create a career that allows you to share your expertise, and then cash in on recommendations based on your experiences. And don't be afraid to get into a niche where you're *not* an expert, too.

Many people love learning right alongside others, so you can start a blog and share your own journey of learning something new, letting your readers see your successes and setbacks – and they'll still enjoy following your progress and learn with you.

In fact, many people say it takes the pressure off of them and makes them feel more comfortable learning from a fellow newbie rather than from someone who talks over their heads and doesn't seem to remember what it was like and some of the problems encountered when just starting out in something.

Trend-Based Niche Markets

There are some topics that are trendy, and you can make money on those. For example, the Zika virus is big in the news right now at the time of this writing. You could create a specific eBook or POD (print on demand) hard cover book on protecting yourself from mosquito-borne illnesses and launch it to the survival crowd.

You could also create blog posts recommending top protection from mosquito bites. That might include posts on repellants, head nets, bracelets, and even more expensive items like traps – all of which would pay a commission to you. While most of trend markets don't entirely go away, those who get in while the topic is climbing or peaking in popularity will cash in the most. However for most of the trending topics, there will always be some residual interest and possibility for sales.

Evergreen Niche Markets

On the opposite side would be the evergreen niche market. That might be a bit broader topic such as a survival site or a general survival health site where you could recommend things that are *always* on the minds of that demographic. These topics constantly sell well and most likely will keep selling well into the future as they are timeless topics.

Anti-aging, health, fitness and weight management are four examples of evergreen niche markets. There will always be people fighting the aging process, trying to stay well and fit, and trying to manage their weight. But there will also be trend patterns such as a fad diet like paleo or low carb, which allows your profits to spike temporarily in these same niches.

Merging Niches for Broader Appeal

Another cool way to pick a niche is to merge topics! For example, anti-aging and weight management can be easily combined - or golf for fitness. You could merge things like gardening and stress relief, and that opens the door to all sorts of stress management and gardening products you could promote.

However, make sure there's some sort of logical connection between the two. For example, don't just stick cooking and anti-aging on the same site. If you specifically want to share cooking *for* anti-aging, with herbs and foods that turn back the clock, then that's fine!

Or, don't even merge niches – just keep it broad like, "Cooking" and then you can cover all sorts of cooking – cooking for:

- Weight loss
- 1-2 people
- Dinner parties
- Cooking for the Holidays
- Food allergies
- Picky eaters
- Crockpot cooking
- Grilling out

- Cast iron cooking…and so on

By keeping it broad, you never paint yourself into a corner with too few topics to discuss, and each blog post on your site serves as an entry point for someone to get to know you, your lessons and buy your books or products you are endorsing.

Drilling Down to Dominate a Narrow Niche

Of course, you might start out thinking in terms of a broad topic, like fishing or golf. But to some, it may seem overwhelming trying to teach all of that – or maybe you just have a specific and narrowed interest in the topic.

You can narrow down and position yourself as the go to person for a smaller demographic, searching for information that suits *their* needs, rather than everyone, everywhere.

So for instance, you could do a narrow site on each of these topics:

- Getting rid of (or minimizing) wrinkles
- Cooking for Diabetics
- Bass Fishing
- Improving Your Short Game (for golfers)
- Raising Chickens (or homesteaders)

You can also start out with a broad site, see which topics you end up enjoying most, and branch off into smaller topics each with their own site over time. That way, if they're all connected, your audience can easily find more good information shared by you in a similar topic.

For example, someone might come in on your anti-wrinkle site, and like what they see – so when they see a link back to your main anti-aging site, they might click there and go read about whatever you have to offer in terms of information on fitness for aging individuals, brain health and more. Anchor linking is a good way to connect sites together, is easy to do and quite effective. Basically you embed the URL of another website into a word that is on one of your other websites. When they click on the anchor word, they end up on your other website.

The great thing about brainstorming a good niche is that you have the opportunity to build as few or as many sites as you can keep up with. And if you get started with one and find out it's not right for you, you can sell it or delete it and move on to something else!

And some of your sites may be static in that once you have them up and running, they will require little to no maintenance to keep them running. Other sites may be changing all the time and require you to do more maintenance to keep things fresh and exciting.

Getting Your Website Up and Running

Once you decide on a niche, it will be time to build a home on the "net" so that you can share information and welcome an audience who will grow loyal to your teachings. You'll do that by buying a domain name and getting a service to host you files, which ends up being your website.

The best (and easiest) system of conveying information is with a simple blog using Wordpress, so we'll talk about what to consider when you set up your blog online and begin inviting people to read what you have to say.

Getting a Domain of Your Own

A domain name is the address where your website will be found. For instance, http://www.YourDomain.com. Some people will say it's okay to go with a .net or .org domain extension, but it's always best to go with a .com domain because that's what most people remember to type in. But if you can't find an available .com domain in your niche, then you may have to look at other extension options.

As for what the domain address will be, you have a few choices. You can brand your own name (in my case RonKness.com), create a catchy name or go with a keyword-based domain. A keyword is a word or phrase that's relevant to your niche topic.

So for example, these are catchy domain ideas:

==> PioneerPatty.com might be great for a woman teaching survivalists to learn old fashioned homesteading

==> GridlessGuy.com might be a brand domain for a guy who teaches you to live off the grid

==> SassySaver.com might be a woman teaching couponing to save money…and so on

But when you have domains like that, sometimes it's hard for people to know just by the name, what your site entails. So it's often best to go with a keyword-based domain, which would be something like this:

==> SurvivalForKids.com – a site teaching parents how to ensure their children are ready for a survival situation

==> SaveYourMarriage.com – a site that shares tips on rekindling the love between spouses

==> AntiAgingBeautyTips.com – a site that focuses on the beauty element of anti-aging

So first, brainstorm some common keyword phrases in your niche topic. Some words that people often use along with their keyword phrases are:

- Tips

- Guide

- News

- Best

- Top

So if you go to Godaddy.com, NameCheap.com or another site that sells domains, you can type in a domain name you're considering to see if it's available. Usually returned will be a list of domain names representative of the domain you wanted. An exact match may or may not be listed. If an exact match is not listed, it means someone else has already purchased it.

Once you buy a particular domain name, nobody else can use that same domain name until you decide to stop using it by not renewing your domain name and then it would be released for someone else to buy.

If you start with AntiAging.com, you'll probably find that someone already owns it. But they may not own BestAntiAgingTips.com, for example. Play around with the name and see what you can come up with. There are free (and paid) keyword tools that will do the brainstorming for you if you get stuck.

Once you find something that you feel represents the broad or narrow slant that you want, you can buy it. Here's a money savings tip: Go to Google and type in the month and year and then the words *GoDaddy.com coupon*.

This should pull up a variety of coupons that take the cost of your domain from $12 to just $1.99 or less. Other domain sellers may have coupons too, so don't forget to look online for those! Just know that when you get ready to renew your domain name, the price will be much higher, but still not exorbitant. Most of my domain names after the first year were no more than $14.00 per year. You can pay for a whole year with just one sale.

Hosting is a bit more confusing for many people. Go with a big name like Hostgator, Blue Host or another provider that has good reviews from other users. If they have 24/7 help available so much the better as this decreases the amount of frustration you'll have if something goes wrong or you feel stuck. Most hosting providers have chat rooms set up so you can get help fairly quickly.

Your host usually charges for a full year up-front right off the bat, but the amount monthly when divided by 12 is usually low. You can get hosting for well under $10 a month and this is where all of your site's files will be housed so that when a visitor goes to your domain, the information presented to them on your behalf comes from your files on this site.

Ask the hosting agent for the smallest package that gives you one site to start with. You can level up with more than one site later if you want, but that will save you a few extra dollars per month and get you started with one site.

Once you have hosting, you'll have to log in to your domain registrar and "point" the servers to your new host. There are many tutorials on exactly how to do this for each hosting company, so just Google it. If you get stuck, call the host or domain registrar and have them walk you through it over the phone.

Basically you need the server names of your host which you'll see on your host account page. Once you have that information, go into your domain account and put the host server names in where it shows the name servers. They normally want two name server names. Usually within 24 hours the name servers are set and your blog is live.

Using a Blog as Your Home Base

WordPress is the best blog platform for you to use for your site. It allows you to easily create pages where you sell products and post blogs where you give on-going tips and advice or make recommendations.

When you log into your hosting account via cpanel, you'll see the option for a QuickInstall of WordPress. Just follow the directions and it will deliver the login URL (usually http://www.yourdomain.com/wp-admin) and you can get started blogging!

There are step-by-step videos online that you can watch if you need some hand holding, but the system walks you through it easily. When your blog is live, go through the settings and choose how you want your blog to perform.

For example, you'll choose how many posts you want it to show on the main page, whether or not people can leave comments, and even how you want each post to look in the URL (the web address) of your site by the theme you choose for your site!

You can select from a wide array of free WordPress themes, and each one has a unique layout of text and images. You can also find paid themes online if you prefer to buy something specific. I've used both free and paid, and the free are just as good in my opinion. Choose something like a Twenty-Fourteen or Twenty-Fifteen or another one that comes as part of your Wordpress install and your site will look great.

Each theme lets you do a preview before you select so you get an idea of how your site will look. You can even change themes after creating your site, but you may have to "massage" some of your existing information to make it look right if it doesn't switch over correctly to the new theme. Because of this, it is best to take the time and select the theme you want in the first place when setting up your site, thus saving time later having to redo stuff if you change themes.

You can create a nice header yourself or, if you don't have any graphic experience, hire someone on a site like Fiverr to make a header for you that is representative of your niche that includes images and text that reflect your topic as well as the name of your site.

Don't make the mistake of trying to set up the perfect blog right off the bat. Keep it simple, not overloaded with plugins or other bells and whistles. It will load faster this way and give you fewer problems. The more plug-ins you use, the more chance of two or more of them "not playing well together", thus giving you problems. As you learn the ropes of how to run a WordPress blog, you can implement more advanced strategies over time.

Building a List of Loyal Subscribers

There are some niche markets where it may be less critical if you build a list of subscribers or not. For example, if someone is buying a tangible item such as a toy for their grandchild once every major holiday like Christmas and birthdays is not as critical as you may only make contact with them a couple times per year.

But with most niche markets, there are multiple selling opportunities, so that means you want to have the visitor's name and email address so you can follow up with more tips and advice – as well as promotions to offer.

If you have a site on countertop blenders, for example, you can still promote things to this list that are relevant, if not specifically about the item they purchased. You can promote cookbooks, accessories, and other kitchen appliances they might be interested in.

What Can a List Do for You?

A list of subscribers means you don't have to continue working hard for every single sale you get. If you fail to build a list, then you're constantly shuffling around online trying to get traffic to your blog so you can earn a commission.

If you capture the name and email addresses from visitors instead, then you can simply blast out an email (using your autoresponder) that informs and educates your subscribers about something, and maybe offers insight on an item they might wish to buy.

The only thing you have to remember is that it's a privilege to be given access to someone's email inbox, so you have to treat the subscribers wonderfully so that you aren't seen as intrusive and annoying. There is a fine line between keeping your name in front of them and harassing them with constant emails.

Usually sending out an email weekly, every two weeks or even just monthly is sufficient. You can schedule the emails in your autoresponder so they are sent automatically at a certain interval in days or at a specific time on a specific day of the week.

Which Email Autoresponder Should You Choose?

There are many email autoresponder services online. Some are free, or have free starter options, and others are paid services. You want something you can grow with over time.

If you absolutely don't have the budget for an email autoresponder, then get started with a free autoresponder like Mail Chimp. However once your subscriber base gets to a certain level, even it turns into a paid subscription. But if you can spend under $20 a month, go with a paid professional service such as Aweber, GetResponse, or others.

Normally, these services have you level up over time. So for instance, on Aweber, it might be $19 a month for up to 500 subscribers, but you get unlimited email sending abilities.

As you grow to 2,500 and 5,000 or more subscribers, your rates go up slightly. That isn't a problem, though, because the list will allow you to make more profits, so the autoresponder ends up more than paying for itself.

Tips for Setting Up Your List and Emails

Whenever you go through the process of setting up your email autoresponder, make sure you provide a P.O. Box as the address or else it will show your home address to everyone who subscribes to your list.

Make sure you go in and set up a welcome email for your new subscribers that they will receive automatically after they confirm their email address. You want to use a system that makes them confirm their subscription permission.

Most autoresponders call it double opt-in. A subscriber first opts-in by requesting whatever it is you are offering. By having to confirm that request is the second opt-in. The confirm email they receive is also sent automatically once you have everything in your autoresponder set which takes minimal amount of time. Once they click on the confirm link, then their first welcome email is sent out.

What can take some time is the email you create that will be sent to a subscriber automatically at the interval you specify, called a follow-up. But once you set up a follow-up sequence of emails, you don't have to do anything with them unless something in your offer changes.

In your welcome email, make sure you share the link to whatever opt-in gift you offered, like a short report, so they have another way to get what you promised them. They should have received a link to the report when they clicked on the confirm email link too.

Invite the reader to contact you if and when they need help, and give them a link or instructions on how to do that. On your website, one of the pages you should have is a Contact Us page. This usually has a web form they can fill out and submit online, along with an email address they can use to contact you by email.

Set up your opt-in form (called a squeeze page or landing page) for your offer on the sidebar of your blog, and share it at the bottom of each blog post that pertains to that offer topic as well. You can have, or make it yourself, a little eCover if you're giving away a short report, and have that positioned either right above the opt-in form on your blog or in your form depending on the autoresponder you choose. Some let you use that image as a background on your squeeze or landing page.

When it comes time to use your email list, you'll log in and choose between a follow-up or broadcast email. A follow-up email is good if you want new subscribers to automatically receive the email sequence you have set up for that product.

But if it's something that might be temporary, like a coupon for a sale, that wouldn't go into your follow up series because it will eventually expire, and people six months down the road that are new to your list would get an expired promo code when they receive that email in the sequence. These time sensitive emails are called broadcast emails as you have to send them out; they don't go out automatically like follow-ups do.

Broadcast emails are emails that go out to everyone on your list at that time you send them. But people who join months or years (or even days) down the road wouldn't see these emails unless you choose to send them to new subscribers. Some people strictly use broadcast emails while others strictly use follow-up emails. Actually once you get into email marketing, you'll find yourself using both types.

If you do use follow-up emails, make sure everything stays up to date. If a link gets broken or a site gets deleted, you'll want to make sure you edit and repair it in that email so that future subscribers don't get a broken link. That can turn off a new subscriber quicker than anything else. Number one priority should be taking care of the customer!

Blogging to Bring Visitors to Your Site

As you embark on your journey to lead a niche market, you'll need to share ideas and thoughts as well as opinions and news on your new blog platform. Some people always ask how they can get traffic pushed to a new site.

A better way to look at this is to work on how you can *pull* traffic into your site, using creative and valuable content that gets posted to your blog. Make sure you don't stick with only using text content.

A good variety of images and videos will help break up the text and make your blog more interactive. You can get images to use on your blog using stock photo sites. Some of the best pay and free ones are:

- iStockPhoto.com – A site where you pay to use the images and there are thousands of stock photos in many sizes that you can use.

- DepositPhotos.com – The same as iStockPhoto – choose amid a wide array of niche pictures.

- MorgueFile.com – A free stock photo site where you don't have to pay, but you may need to give credit to the photographer, so make sure you check the rules for each photo.

- Pixabay.com – Like MorqueFile, it is free also and most images do not require attribution (crediting the photographer), but read the license to be sure.

Don't worry about investing in larger photos unless you are going to offer a printed version of your book. Then you'll need images that are at least 300 dpi (dots per inch). Otherwise, small images at 72 ppi (pixels per inch) will be plenty big enough for a blog post that will only be seen on a computer monitor. You can then write your post, and about halfway down, embed the image or place it in the upper left-hand corner of your blog right before the start of your text.

If you choose to have an image representative of you, verses a product, you can include your brand image in each email. As far as blog post, your brand image can be part of your website header. After a while, your customers and readers will recognize your brand image and know the information is from you.

Having your brand image in blog posts is also good for when you share the blog post on social networking sites because it will automatically pull the image into the post. It's been proven in research that posts with images get more attention than those without.

So what will you blog about? Let's look at a few ideas to help you brainstorm a list of blog topics. One thing you might want to do is find a printable calendar (or buy one) and jot down potential topics so that each morning, you simply open the calendar and choose the topic.

Or you can write blog posts ahead and schedule them to post on a certain day or time.

The topic you choose should be those that your readers are searching for. So using a good keyword tool (free or paid) is a nice way to discover what your audience needs. For example, if you have a golf blog, and you want to know what those readers are searching for, you might start out by entering the words *golf training* into the keyword tool.

From there, you may see the phrase *golf training balls* so you click on that to "drill down" and see what people specifically want to know. You find the phrase *golf training balls: foam or plastic* and you know that a blog post comparing the two options would be something that your readers might enjoy.

Another thing you can do is post about any breaking news in your niche. For example, if you had a survival site and you wanted to use a news slant, you might choose a current topic like the Zika virus or any sort of economic fluctuation that alarms preppers.

To find out what's in the news for your niche, you can set up what's known as a Google Alert, where each day's news and information hits your inbox on whatever topic is in your alert. Or, you can simply go to Google and type in a keyword or phrase from your niche and click on search and the news tab. It is interesting to either set up an alert or search online for your name to see what (if anything) is being said about you on the Internet.

So for example, if I did type in Zika and clicked the news tab, you would find that the FDA approved the use of mutant mosquitoes that kill Zika-infected mosquitoes. And then of course, your blog post could share the details of the news, while continuing to advise your readers of what to do with the information.

Giving your readers tips in a blog post is a great way to develop loyalty. Blog readers love things like, "7 Ways to Keep Wrinkles at Bay" or "5 Tips for Catching More Bass." Numbered blog posts for tips are very popular.

You can also do step-by-step tip posts. With these, you're sharing a bite-sized snippet of information, such as, "3 Steps to Improve Your Marriage Today." They don't have to be posts with 101 tips. As a matter-of-fact, readers have short attention spans, so you want to keep blog posts short. If you have a blog topic that is long, break it up into two or even three separate posts.

Q&A sessions are an awesome way to bond with your readers. There are a couple of ways you can do this. Obviously, if you have a blog readership, then you can poll (or survey) your readers and find out what questions they have for you or do it as a contest so the winner(s) receive some sort of gift for participating.

Yes it is a little like bribery, but it works. Otherwise participation can be slim, which doesn't always give you enough data to make an informed decision about whatever it is you are polling or surveying.

But what if you're new to blogging and don't yet have anyone to poll? Another good way to conduct a Q&A is to go out and scout out common questions in your niche and answer them yourself.

So your blog post would simply say, "Q&A for FAQ" and you would start off by saying you wanted to address some common questions about survival, or anti-aging, or golf or whatever topic you're blogging about.

You don't need to fib and say they're questions that came in from your readers. Be truthful at all times with your audience and they will appreciate the transparency and develop loyalty to you for that.

Another good blog post to make is just about your personal journey within the niche. Cover common struggles you've had, successes (big and small) and mindset evolutions.

Reviewing Products as an Affiliate

Everything you've done to this point has been based on the required technical and strategic steps you have to take to set up a thriving business online. Now it's time to discover how you can monetize your efforts.

One of the easiest ways to earn profits online using your blog and email system is to review other people's products. This can be a mix of tangible and digital products, depending on your niche – or it might be one or the other.

Pick Your Products Carefully

It's never a good idea to choose products based solely on what's on the bestseller list. Although this does indicate a hefty interest and profitability, there have been known duds that get top billing, and you can easily ruin your reputation as a quality niche leader if you blindly recommend random products.

Whether the product is digital or tangible, you want to choose items whose creators have solid reputations. Brand names matter when it comes to tangible items, and some have better reputations than others.

Likewise, with digital products, you want to promote vendors who have a strong reputation for supporting their buyers and developing top quality information.

Your list expects you to refer them to capable and helpful individuals. Never simply choose a product based on the price tag and potential commission you may earn, either. You will earn more respect (and ultimately, more money) by recommending products based off of the merit of the product or author, not solely on the size of the commissions.

Hands On Reviews of Tangibles

Tangible items are fun to review and if you can buy one once in a while; they make great reviews for video. People love to see products in action, even if it's just you taking something out of the box and discussing it called an unboxing review .

All you do is wait for your product to be delivered and then turn on the camera and record your reactions to what you think as you bring the product out of the box and discuss its features and accessories that come with it.

If possible, and the product allows for it, then do an instant review of yourself using the product at that time. Or, promise you'll use it and get back to the reader with a follow-up video.

There are many places to find tangible items that you can promote. Amazon is very popular, but it's not the only place. You can go to Commission Junction and Share-a-Sale and even sign up directly with sites like Target, Walmart and more to earn commissions.

Implementation Reviews of Digitals

Digital products are a bit harder to review in one sitting. Information usually has to be applied in order to work – even a book you have to first read before doing a review. It might take two or more series of blog posts to fully review as can be the case with software.

Go through the buying process on day 1 and then from then on implement the ideas found in the digital course and discuss the results. Don't give away the product owner's message to your viewers – but discuss how it's working for you, including things you don't like about it.

There are many places you can go to find good digital courses to promote in your niche. Some of the more popular ones include ClickBank, JVZoo and Warrior Plus. All of these have a variety of niche products.

Don't discount the promotion of Amazon Kindle reads, though. You won't get as much commission off of them, but if you pair the promotion with tangible items, such as an anti-aging eBook with supplements or beauty products, it can boost your bottom line quickly.

Promotions Versus Reviews

There's a big difference between reviewing a product and simply promoting one. A review is where you actually have access to the product and you're giving insight into your experiences with it.

In certain cases, it's possible to review a product thoroughly with details and opinions, even if you haven't held it or implemented it yourself. But in those cases, make sure your readers know what angle you're speaking from.

A promotion is nothing more than the blast of a link and encouragement to buy something, even if you aren't familiar with it – what benefits it offers, how it works, etc. Promotions should only be reserved for rare moments when you have full trust in the seller and you're transparent about the fact that you haven't had a chance to check it out personally, but you're aware of the reputation of the seller.

Tips on Making the Most Out of Your Blog Reviews

Blog posts for reviews should be thorough. You want to cover benefits, drawbacks, features and more. If something is generally good, but may have a less than desirable feature, be transparent and make note of what you don't like about the product.

Otherwise when your readers buy it and discover the issue, they will wonder why you didn't mention it. Your readers have put their trust in you – don't do anything that could break that bond. Go into the various uses for the product and if possible, detail your own experiences.

In some cases, you'll find reviews from others who have something negative to say. If this is a case where you have a solution for that problem, go ahead and discuss it (along with your advice on how to fix it).

Use a mix of text and video, but don't forget to use images, too. Many vendors will allow affiliates to use banner ads that they create for you, or use the product image in your blog post. Some vendors will even create sample emails called swipes that you can use for promoting their products. Just insert your own link and you are done.

Make sure you link using a text hyperlink as well as link the image to the product. You never know how your audience will attempt to click through and you want to cover all bases.

Some people focus all of their time on how long the blog post should be – is 400 words better, or 800 words? The correct answer is, *as long as it needs to be*. Don't try adding fluff and filler, but don't skimp on the information either.

Developing an Info Product to Sell

Creating your own information product to sell as both a digital and printable book (in the case of Createspace.com's print on demand (POD)), is a great way to brand yourself as an authority figure *and* earn extra money!

People are always looking for information on a topic, and they want to buy from multiple sources – not just one. They're looking for nuggets of information not found in other books, as well as different styles of presentation.

For example, have you ever read a book that felt too stuffy for you? Maybe it was too technical or scientific. There are books on health topics that are like this, and there are the more consumer-friendly reads that speak in a more casual and conversational manner.

Personality goes a long way in setting you apart from the masses. For example, in the diet niche, you can find all sorts of info products, such as:

- Books that are slanted to scientifically explain what happens to your body when you consume different foods

- Books that are written in a drill sergeant, boot camp manner to kick your rear into action and make you put down that donut and pick up a salad

- Books that are written from a loving standpoint that feel very emotionally motivating and gentle where it coddles you into loving yourself through the nutritional mistakes that you make

- Books that are humorous in nature and make you feel like you can relate to the situation and laugh about it, such as dealing with an uncomfortable naysayer in a funny way

So don't worry about competition. Even mothers-to-be will gobble up dozens of parenting books before the baby is even born – and consumers usually want to invest in multiple viewpoints. And if someone likes your work, they will be back for more.

Decide on a Series Versus a Solo Book

There are two ways you can approach this. You can write a thorough, comprehensive book with a high page count. Or you can divide your concept up into bite-sized pieces and write shorter books for each one of them thus creating a series.

A series often does well on sites like Amazon in the Kindle section. But you can do both if you want to. For example, you might have a big book on Reversing the Anti-Aging Process and then smaller books on specific anti-aging topics, such as:

- Preventing Dementia

- Keeping Your Mobility Intact

- Reversing Hearing Loss

- Diabetes Care for Seniors

- …and more!

Both with Amazon and Createspace, and probably others, you can connect all books together in a series easily. For example, I have five books in a series on both Createspace and Draft2Digital called Healthy Lifestyle Reports: one each on Senior Health, Nutrition, Fitness, Weight Management and Fat-Burning/Motivation.

While a series is usually associated with fiction, as you can see, it doesn't have to be, non-fiction works also.

Do Your Research and Write

The key is to first brainstorm everything you want to cover off the top of your head. Doing this allows you to ensure you're not going to forget to include something you felt was important. I like to use the old-fashion outlining that you learned how to do in school. It capsulizes and organizes what I want to say in my book, thus making it easier to write as one chapter flows into the other.

Then start researching. Go into Amazon in the books section and find other books on your topic. Click on the "Look Inside" feature and go straight to the Table of Contents.

See what topics are discussed and jot them down.

For example, you may have forgotten to list something like eye wrinkles or age spots in your anti-aging book. This exercise will help jog your memory so that your books are comprehensive in nature.

You never want to copy from someone else's books. Just research what issues need to be covered. It also helps if you go into the book's reviews and read through the lower rated ones.

Consumers will often tell you if important information is missing (or wrong) and you can make note of it for your future release, so that you meet their needs right out of the gate!

Get a Professional Cover

Some people try to make their own cover, and while it saves money, it can also prevent you from making money. Consumers don't want to buy a book from an amateur. They want to buy a book from a professional.

So invest about $50-70 in having a professional cover made so that your book will sell many copies. A cover should never cost thousands of dollars. That's for professional publishing houses, not an indie-published author like you or me. However, if you have some graphic creative talents or have taken desktop publishing courses, you can design your own.

I use a program called KDRenegade that makes creating professional-style covers easy. Just pick a template and change the image, along with the words to reflect your title, subtitle and name as the author.

You can download an image from one of the stock photo sites mentioned in s previous chapter or use one of your own photos for your book cover. If you do decide to hire it done from a site like Fiverr, send the image to your cover designer and tell then you need a cover created around that image for a particular niche.

Make sure you send them examples of professional covers that you think are good. That way, they can design something along the same lines. And look for patterns in the designs that are on the bestseller list in your niche category because there may be some things that attract consumers more than others.

Publish Online

You have several options about where you can publish. Many people choose Amazon Kindle because Amazon sells more eBooks than anything else on its site. It's a trusted, household brand, too – so consumers aren't wary of completing a transaction there.

You have the option of only publishing digitally, or using a site called Createspace to also publish a print on demand version of your book. Many consumers prefer holding a physical book in their hands rather than reading an eBook.

Amazon Kindle also has a program called Matchbook, where if they buy one of your printed books they can get the eBook for lesser price than if they would have purchased just the eBook separatey. You can opt for that program by checking the box at the point in the book upload process that talks about Matchbook.

In Createspace, you can choose to get your book listed on Amazon, along with several other places in addition to Createspace, by selecting it as one place you want your book to be listed. My non-fiction POD books sell better on Createspace than anywhere else, but fiction eBooks sell better on Amazon.

Your professional cover designer can usually create a print cover in addition to a digital one for you and it will add on a bit to the expense. You can always go back later and do this part if you want to start with a digital option only at first.

Another way to publish yourself is to publish the book on your own domain and use a platform like JVZoo.com or ClickBank.com to process the payments through PayPal or credit cards. Or you can create a Buy button in PayPal and have customers order directly from your site. This cuts out the middleman and gives you a little more profit from each sale. However if you are going to use affiliates to help sell your product, then going through one of the platforms mentioned makes tracking and paying commissions easier.

To sell a book off of your site, you need to have a sales page ready for your eBook, to explain its benefits and how it will provide a solution to your readers. The good thing about this is that you can often charge more for digital eBooks listed on your site (such as $27) compared to a $2.99 Kindle book). Just don't list your eBook in both places at drastically different prices. With Amazon's marketing power, you may actually make more money with them selling more copies at a lower price ... at least until you get a customer base of your own

But the drawback is, it's up to you to get traffic to it, whereas on Amazon Kindle, your book is built into a system already filled with potential customers, so your job would be to promote the book in other ways or just let Amazon promote it for you for free just from their massive customer base and marketing plan.

You can stay on top of the latest news and publish books online that will take advantage of early trends. For example, if you were in the financial health niche, and you saw the Greece situation brewing, you could have create a book about what to do in case of economic collapse and capitalize on the trend and news.

Recruiting Affiliates and Joint Venture Partners

It's not difficult to make money online, but it's a whole lot easier having a slew of others behind you, sending their customers and traffic to your offers to help you do it! Affiliates and joint venture partners are basically one in the same.

But joint venture partners might have a bit more say in terms of perks and benefits of the promotion. Anyone who is an affiliate can sign up for your product to promote it for a standard commission, assuming you approve them.

But with joint venture partners, the deals can be made behind the scenes to give them perks that other regular affiliates don't enjoy. You want to open the doors to affiliates and also court top JV partners in your quest to make money online.

What Your Affiliates Need

Your job is to put your product on the market and entice affiliates to sign up to promote it for you. But they'll need certain details and information, so let's cover some of the more common aspects of that process.

First, they need the specific information about what's in your product. Detail every element of it – the type of product (audio, eBook, etc.), how many pages or minutes or hours it is total, and what it teaches.

You don't have to give away all of the information about how to do what it teaches, but just cover what their buyers will learn when they invest in your product.

They also need to know exact launch times. If you have a sale going on for a certain period of time, such as a week-long discount, then you need to specify what date and time (and time zone) that it starts and ends. In today's world, many affiliates create bonuses exclusively to a product they are promoting.

If you have a contest running for your affiliates, where those who make the most sales wins money or prizes, then you also need to specify any minimum limitations, prize amounts, and other details.

Make sure you include where they should go to get their affiliate link. You might give them the affiliate page URL on JVZoo, or provide a URL with XXXXX where their username will go if it's a ClickBank product, for example so they can just fill that in easily.

What Your Affiliates Want

Some vendors go a little advanced with what they provide to their affiliates, so you have to understand that to be competitive, it's in your best interest to provide for the wants of the affiliates, and not just the necessities.

Swipe files are a good thing to add to your affiliate or JV page. A swipe file is basically a promotion email pre-written by you that your affiliates can cut and paste into their email autoresponder to promote your product to their list.

It gives all the pertinent information, detailing the product itself – but you'll simply put "INSERT LINK" wherever the affiliate is supposed to paste their unique affiliate link into the swipe file.

Some vendors do a variety of swipe files, such as long emails or short ones, emails detailing the product or those making it somewhat mysterious to get the click-through, and emails that are strategic for the start of a launch versus the last 24 hours for urgency.

Bonus landing pages are another perk you can offer to affiliates who look for vendors who do a little more than the minimum for them. This is where you have one or more bonuses for your customers, and the affiliates can use a landing page that looks like the bonuses are a special deal for their customers.

Early bird discounts are a perk, too. Affiliates love it when they can tell their customers that from 9-11 AM, for example, the product will be on an even steeper discount than the length of the main sale, which could last 4-7 days.

Many affiliates appreciate notification about the launch with enough time to create a bonus of their own. Having an exclusive bonus to provide a list when you promote someone's product helps you bring in more sales, and with plenty of time, they can be very competitive for the customers who buy through links based on bonus choices.

Going Above and Beyond for Your JV Partners

Your prime joint venture partners deserve a little extra care and attention. These are the top affiliates who bring in a lot of traffic and sales. Exclusive bonuses for their list can be a great incentive for them to promote you – because it means they don't have to work on a bonus themselves. But make sure it's exclusive only for them.

Increased commission of 75-100% from the usual 50% are also a welcomed perk among top joint venture partners. Many refuse to promote on the sale level, and if you have one or more one-time offers on the backend, then you can afford to offer 100% on the front end product. Some people wonder why they would offer 100% commission if they are not going to make anything from the sale themselves. The money for them is in the upsells, downsells and additional offers.

Some sellers reduce the percent of commission after the front-end offer while others keep the percentage the same to build their lists. All the buyers from a JV or affiliate's list that bought your offer are now aware of your website, so the next time you promote something they might buy it direct from you.

Some vendors also provide an early, closed promotion period just for their JV partners. So for instance, for the first 48 hours, close JVs get to promote solo, and then it opens for the rest of the affiliates.

Coaching Others in Exchange for Pay

As you begin developing a taste for Internet marketing, and your advice becomes more sought out by the paying public, you might consider going into the branch of business known as online coaching.

There are coaches for many different types of niches, including:

- Dating and relationships
- Debt and credit repair
- Fitness and health
- Career choices and success
- …even things like playing guitar!

If someone will pay for the information, then chances are, they'll be willing to pay for one-on-one coaching or even group coaching that gives them direct access to you so they can pick your brain a little and get feedback.

This is much better than simply downloading an e-course or buying a physical book and not having the ability to ask questions. Some marketers run a membership site as a coaching site.

Your Only Prerequisite

You can create a blog, promote products, and even craft eBooks about your niche topic. But you shouldn't attempt coaching without some level of success already under your belt.

Someone who is failing to succeed in relationships, fitness, finances, or music shouldn't be attempting to teach others (and worse – charge them for it) until they've mastered the set of skills beforehand.

Even if you're overweight by 100 pounds, but you've lost the first 25 pounds, that's enough of a record to let people know you're succeeding. Always be honest about your qualifications when it comes to coaching.

The Use of Live Forms of Communication

Some forms of coaching mean your coaching client will want live interaction with you. Using a free tool like Skype, coaches can now connect to their clients one-on-one using immediate text or video streams. Others will use various webinar program to produce webcasts. If watched live, viewers also have the opportunity to ask questions and get answers during the live broadcast. Of course they can also listen to the replay, but won't have the live question option.

This allows you to coach people all around the globe, without having to spend money to connect to them. You might also have a phone call with your coaching clients, and you can charge by the minute, hour or sell it in bulk packages for a certain amount of calls.

Group Coaching Options

Sometimes people don't want one-on-one coaching. It can be too intimidating to them – or it's too costly. You can also host group coaching for your clients, depending on the topic.

For example, you could have a credit repair or weight loss coaching group. The smaller the group, the better – but some group coaching involves hundreds of participants. The expectations are lower for these in terms of having hands on access to the coach.

You can host group coaching in a private Facebook group, in a membership area set up on a site that you own, or even through the use of private blog posts right on your blog, where you simply password protect the posts.

Successful Coaching

Whatever you do, you don't want to disappoint your coaching clients. They've paid for whatever access and instructions you promised, so make sure that you uphold those promises.

Part of what makes coaching successful is in helping your client determine their goals. These could be both long and short term goals. People often get overwhelmed in the very beginning of their journey because they set unrealistic goals, such as something too big or doing something in too short of a time span.

Once you've assisted them in goal setting, work on helping them pinpoint their common problem areas. If it's dieting, then maybe they're emotional eaters. Or perhaps pre-planning meal is the real issue.

As you help them analyze their problems and work on solutions, just make sure you keep steering them toward final success. Sometimes that means pushing them out of their comfort zone to the next level.

But in the end, their solution has to be theirs if they are to take ownership of it. Otherwise, if it is your solution and they fail, they will blame you.

Supplementing Senior Income as a Service Provide

Sometimes, the thought of starting your own business from scratch is overwhelming. This is especially true if you're used to working for someone else all these years. Many retirees will welcome the entrepreneurial role, while others just want to fill their time with tasks and earn compensation for it.

One option for you to get started making money quickly, without having to go through the task of launching a website and products, is to work as a service provider. Service providers handle tasks for other online marketers who already have a thriving business.

Perks of Working for Someone Else

With this type of startup business, you can hit the ground running. All you have to do is seek out people needing whatever skills you have to offer, and apply for the job! Most of these jobs are one-time tasks, but some can turn into long-term assignments if you find someone you enjoy working with (and they visa-versa).

Keep in mind that you have full control over who you have as a client. You can enjoy the perks of working with more than one client at a time, if you have enough hours in the day.

There's no overhead or expenses you have to pay. Typically, the only money you'll be paying out is the fee charged by platforms where you find this work, and PayPal taking their cut of your income.

But those are usually nominal fees and the great news is, they don't get paid until you actually get a paying gig. In some cases, such as on sites like UpWork, you might have a small fee to have a profile and be able to bid on more jobs.

Opportunities for Service Providers

So what types of things are considered to be service provider jobs? There are four major ones you can look into, and then you can also find other opportunities just by knowing where to look.

The first is what's known as a virtual assistant (VA). Consider this similar to an executive secretary of sorts, but all your work is done online. You'll be handling a wide variety of tasks, and in most cases, you'll need to be knowledgeable (or willing to learn) about online tasks, like handling files.

VAs typically write emails (some both as replies to ones send from customers and autoresponder follow-ups and broadcasts), handle help desk requests, write sales pages, posts blogs, upload files to the hosting account, etc.

Another opportunity might be ghostwriting for others. If you can write in the same vein as this course, in a conversational manner, then you'll be a great fit to write someone's niche content, such as blog posts, articles, reports, eBooks, and more. For example in addition to writing both ebooks and PODs, I also contract ghostwrite 15 health and fitness articles monthly for a marketer in England and a weekly column for a job search site.

Another option is to work as a graphic designer for someone. Graphic designers are needed to create website headers, eBook covers, infographics and social media quote posters, to name a few.

You can also find work handling customer service emails. Many top marketers have help desks where the customer creates a support ticket. Then you would go in and find a solution to their problem, such as a missing file or sign up error.

Where to Find Service Provider Jobs

Service provider jobs are all around on what are known as freelance websites. One of the most popular ones is called UpWork, where you can sign up as a service provider and bid on the jobs that you want.

You'll earn a job satisfaction rating and the higher it is, the more likely you are to get hired in the future by other marketers. You'll create a profile detailing all of your expertise and then the marketers will review it and see if you're a good match, at which time they'll hire you.

You can also find work on other marketing hot spots such as WarriorForum.com, where they have a Warriors for Hire area. There are others, but some of them pay very low and you'll want to steer clear of those.

Protect Yourself from Scams

It's not just customers who get taken advantage of online. Service providers do too. Many marketers mistakenly think that they can mistreat freelancers as if they were an employee of their company (which is also wrong).

You'll want to check the feedback of the buyer before bidding on their project. Other service providers have the opportunity to leave a review of the buyer, and they'll tell you if the person paid on time, was difficult to work with – or an absolute dream of a client.

Level Up Your Pay

It's natural, at first, to want to earn a lot of money, fast – especially if you have experience in the field of the job you're bidding on.

But online, the slate is wiped clean and you have to earn a reputation as a quality provider.

Start out bidding competitively, but just slightly under the competition. Don't go too low. After each successful project, raise your prices for the next buyer – and ask your clients to leave good feedback for your job well done.

Ways to Increase Traffic and Sales

Traffic is the lifeblood of your website or offer's success. Without eyeballs on your offers, no one can hire you or download your product or buy off of your recommendation where you make a consistent income.

Some of the efforts you'll tackle will help you pull traffic into your site. Others will require you to get out there and push prospective customers to your sales or landing pages during a launch and beyond.

So let's look at several ways you can stir up interest in whatever it is that you have to offer…

Blogging and Guest Blogging

Blogging is when you create unique articles on your own domain with valuable information and contain your own point of view. You can use keywords in the title and body of your blog content and when Google indexes your site, they can present it to those who go to their search engine and type in those words or phrases.

Blogging is most effective as a means of traffic when you do it consistently – daily, or at the very least, weekly. You want to research your blog posts and ensure that your blogs are up-to-date and different from the masses.

You can also be a guest blogger for other blog owners. This is when you get brought onboard to craft a unique blog post, and you're given a byline within the post that exposes their audience to your name, website URL and a brief blurb about you.

Social Networking

You're probably already a member of various social networking sites like Facebook or LinkedIn. You can join all sorts of niche social networking sites such as Pinterest, Instagram, Snapchat and more.

Using social networks allows you to make friends within the niche community that you hope to lead, providing insight in a free method that leads to them following you on your own domain, where your paid products reside.

Forums are a form of social networking that allow you to participate in solving other people's problems in an open community. Someone posts a problem, you offer your $0.02 worth, and when people enjoy what you had to say, they can access your profile or signature file that contains a link back to your own site.

Viral Multimedia

Viral multimedia isn't always based on something outlandish like a mom laughing hysterically in a Star Wars Chewbacca mask. Sometimes, things can go viral on a smaller scale – within your niche, and they're just as effective as a stunt video, if not more so.

You can create videos that get shared by people – using sites like YouTube or Vimeo. You only need simple equipment, like a smart phone, and you can hit the record button and upload it directly without waiting for editing.

You don't have to use video at all if it feels intimidating to you. You can go viral with other media formats such as images. Images can be used to create what are known as social quote posters.

This is usually a motivating image with an inspiring quote plastered across it. These get viewed and shared a ton on sites like Facebook and Pinterest, whenever people see them in their news feed and like what they have to say. Make sure you brand your website's URL on the image before it goes viral.

Images can also be used to create informative infographics. If you go to Pinterest, you'll see infographics used a lot. They're long, narrow posters of short quick facts and tips within a niche.

Don't forget that not everything relies on a visual stimulation to get a message across. You can use audio podcasting to create a viral effect too.

All you do here is record yourself speaking – just like you're on a radio show, and upload it to iTunes or other platforms. Creating audio versions of your eBooks can be a great way to get another stream of income. This allows you to cater to those that like to listen and learn while commuting to and from work.

Giveaway Events

These traditional methods of traffic generation require you to partner up in many cases with other online marketers, but it's a great way to create a buzz and build your list with new subscribers and visitors to your site.

What you do is contact several marketers in a similar niche to yours (competitors are great for this purpose) and you all develop something small to give away. It could be a short, 5-page report, for example.

Each of you sends traffic to the giveaway single page, which houses a link to each of your offers. When the visitor arrives, they pick and choose whose offers they want and go to that individual's site to sign up to their list to download the offer.

If you're new, you won't have as much traffic to contribute, so you might offer to buy paid traffic in an effort to do your share of bringing in interested parties, while the others can use their own list of subscribers. The advantage is you can get traffic from other peoples' lists and if they like your products, could become regular customers of yours.

Offline Traffic

Sometimes, you can send offline consumers onto the Internet where they can find your blog, sign up to your list and purchase your product. Offline traffic can be done in a myriad of ways, but you don't have to go hand out flyers on car windshields.

One of the best methods for finding offline traffic is to get published offline in what are known as trade magazines. Pick up a copy of your latest Writer's Market book for the current year and look for the trade magazines that fit your niche.

Getting published in a trade magazine is easier than getting published in a mainstream magazine. There's not a lot of pay in it, but that's not your goal anyway. Your goal is to attract the readers to your blog using your byline.

Paid Traffic

This is another option and if done carefully, can provide a rich source of targeted traffic to your blog. Paid traffic can be done in many different avenues. The key is to pay the least amount possible for each click-through to your website.

You can start by purchasing a solo advertisement. A solo ad is basically buying access to a certain number of subscribers on someone else's list.

You'll write an email for the other person to send out to their list, based on their criteria and specifications.

They'll send it out for you and get paid for the email blast. You can often see how a seller is rated (meaning whether or not their list was responsive, or if it fell flat). This is a good way to shop for traffic.

Another way to pay for traffic is to use a tool like Facebook advertising. You can create entire campaigns that are targeted according to gender, location, and interests. So if you want to run an ad to people who love survival, they can target that!

Or if you want to be in the golf niche, target your ad to golfers. You can even target the female golfers over age 60 if you want to. Facebook advertising can be done for a little amount (such as $5 a day) or more, if your campaigns become successful.

Final Thoughts

Making money online as a senior can be a very fun journey if you let it. Resist the temptation to get overwhelmed and try to learn everything in a day – or a week. It won't happen that fast! Take it one step at a time. Rome wasn't built in a day and neither will be your website.

But it is a great way to meet new friends, offer your guidance to others based on your rich experiences, and earn a nice, tidy sum for your insight. It's very freeing being your own boss, and working as an online entrepreneur from home is the icing on the cake!

About the Author

I grew up in Central Minnesota, where my parents owned and operated a fishing resort. Once out of high school I tried a couple of semesters of college, only to quit halfway through the Spring term; I decided at that time that college wasn't for me.

Then I decided to follow my father's previous occupation as an auto mechanic. I graduated from a two-year of vocational training course and worked as a mechanic for five years. While in vocational training, I decided to join the National Guard where I eventually ended up working full-time for 32 years.

So how does all of this relate to writing? In one of my leadership schools, the instructor, who was an English teacher at a juvenile detention center, presented writing to me in a whole new way - a way that started to develop my interest in working with words.

I eventually went back to college on the GI Bill while I was working and earned my Bachelor's degree in Business Administration. Taking a class or two per semester at night and on weekends took me seven years to complete my degree.

Fast forward about 40 years and I now have published over 75 books on Amazon for Kindle, CreateSpace and other publishing platforms.

Besides my own writing, I also ghostwrite ebooks, reports, articles, blogs and do Kindle conversions for clients on a variety of topics.

Today my wife and I are retired from our careers and live in Gold Canyon, AZ. I now write as a retirement business where you'll find me happily sitting in my office typing away on my laptop as I work on my next book or ghostwriting project . . . that is if we are not traveling on a cruise ship - our new-found mode of travel.

www.ingramcontent.com/pod-product-compliance
Lightning Source LLC
Chambersburg PA
CBHW021440170526
45164CB00001B/328